CHANGING
Families

Foster
Families

Carla Mooney

ReferencePoint
Press®

San Diego, CA

About the Author

Carla Mooney is the author of many books for young adults and children. She lives in Pittsburgh, Pennsylvania, with her husband and three children.

For more information, contact:
ReferencePoint Press, Inc.
PO Box 27779
San Diego, CA 92198
www.ReferencePointPress.com

Picture Credits:

Cover: dnf-style/Depositphotos

6: Maury Aaseng
11: Liderina/Shutterstock.com
18: Anurak Pongpatimet/Shutterstock.com
22: Darren Baker/Shutterstock.com

28: Daisy Daisy/Shutterstock.com
33: iStockphoto.com
38: Associated Press
43: Andy Martin Jr./ZUMA Press/Newscom
49: Joe Burbank/KRT/Newscom
53: PeopleImages/iStockphoto.com

LIBRARY OF CONGRESS CATALOGING-IN-PUBLICATION DATA

Names: Mooney, Carla, 1970– author.
Title: Foster Families/by Carla Mooney.
Description: San Diego, CA: ReferencePoint Press, [2019] | Series: Changing Families | Audience: Grade 9 to 12. | Includes bibliographical references and index.
Identifiers: LCCN 2018022786 (print) | LCCN 2018026189 (ebook) | ISBN 9781682823583 (eBook) | ISBN 9781682823576 (hardback)
Subjects: LCSH: Foster parents—Juvenile literature. | Families—Juvenile literature.
Classification: LCC HQ759.7 (ebook) | LCC HQ759.7 .M66 2019 (print) | DDC 306.874—dc23
LC record available at https://lccn.loc.gov/2018022786

Contents

Chapter One

How American Families Are Changing

Over a period of two years, LaToya Cromwell had moved from one foster home to another. At age fifteen, she arrived at the home of Phyllis Wilson, the woman who was to be her foster mother for about a week, until she could be placed in a more permanent group home. But something happened during that week with Wilson. For the first time in a long time, Cromwell felt like she belonged. She felt safe. "I didn't feel like I was in foster care,"[1] she says.

Cromwell moved to the group home as planned but could not forget that feeling of belonging that she experienced with Wilson. She made many phone calls to Wilson, asking if she could move back in with her. And that is what happened; Cromwell moved back to Wilson's home. At the same time, Wilson realized that she, too, had developed a special feeling for this young woman— and she eventually became Cromwell's legal, permanent guardian. Now, at age seventeen, Cromwell has stopped worrying about the next day, the next foster family, the next foster home. Instead, like many high school seniors, she is thinking about college. "Having her as a parent, it's the structure that I need to do what I need to do," says Cromwell. "But then there's also flexibility and love, the understanding part."[2]

Foster care is not new to Wilson. For more than a decade, she has fostered children of all ages. Some have stayed for a few nights, and others have stayed longer. Wilson, who is a divorced single mom with two grown biological children and one adopted child, says that each child who comes through her door becomes one of her own, no matter how long they stay. She tucks them in at night, helps them with their homework, makes sure they eat enough, and gives them plenty of hugs. "Everything that I did for my children that I bore, I have done for the children I've taken in," she says. "The exact same thing." Wilson describes herself as the children's godmother. "I always tell them: 'You know, God put us together. Because you needed a little help and I'm going to

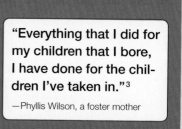

help your parents. That makes me your godmother,'"[3] she says. Wilson and Cromwell are an example of one type of changing American family: a foster family.

What Is Foster Care?

Foster care is a temporary living arrangement for children when their birth parents cannot care for them. A foster care arrangement can be informal, or it can be arranged by the courts or a social service agency. When a child needs a temporary living arrangement, caseworkers often first look to find a family member who can take the child into their home and provide care. However, many children who enter foster care do not have relatives available to provide care. In these cases, social service agencies find nonrelative foster families, who are often strangers to the child. Foster families agree to care for the child and give him or her a safe place to live. They attempt to provide children as normal a home life as possible. In some cases, children in foster care may live in group settings with other foster children. In a group home, several foster children live together with staff members, often called house parents, who work in shifts at the home. Other group settings for foster children include shelters and residential treatment centers, which help children who are dealing with mental illness or other health problems.

The immediate goal of foster care is to make sure that a child has a stable, safe place to live. Foster care is only intended to be temporary. Its primary goal is to eventually reunite a child with his or her birth parent or parents once they are able to take care of the

Foster Youth Live in a Variety of Settings

Young people in foster care are placed in a variety of settings. These include homes of relatives, homes of nonrelatives, and group homes—among others. As of September 30, 2016, an estimated 437,465 young people were in foster care nationwide. Most of them, 45 percent, lived in the homes of people who were not relatives. Another 32 percent lived with a relative who provided foster care. These are the two most common home settings for foster youth.

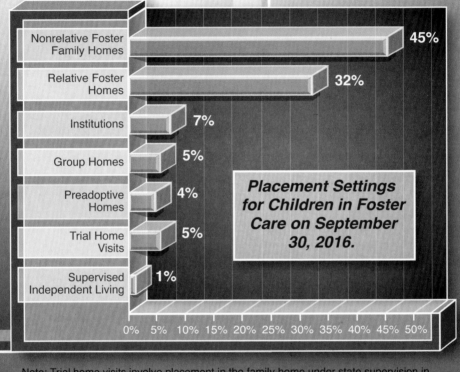

Placement Settings for Children in Foster Care on September 30, 2016.

Setting	Percent
Nonrelative Foster Family Homes	45%
Relative Foster Homes	32%
Institutions	7%
Group Homes	5%
Preadoptive Homes	4%
Trial Home Visits	5%
Supervised Independent Living	1%

Note: Trial home visits involve placement in the family home under state supervision in preparation for family reunification.

Source: US Department of Health and Human Services, Children's Bureau, Child Welfare Information Gateway, "Foster Care Statistics 2016," April 2018. www.childwelfare.gov.

child. "Reuniting or preventing a child from entering foster care is always our number one goal,"[4] says Jerry Milner, the acting commissioner for the Administration for Children, Youth, and Families (ACF). Once a birth parent is back on track—or another relative or guardian steps forward to care for the child—the child returns to his or her family. According to the US Department of Health and

Human Services (HHS), approximately three out of five children in foster care return home to live with birth parents or other relatives. By law, children in foster care are supposed to have contact with their birth family—parents and siblings—through regular visits.

Most of the time, reunification with a birth family does not happen quickly. Instead, it can take weeks or months to reunite children with their birth families. Under federal law, states must create a permanency plan for every child in foster care. This plan outlines where the child will live when he or she leaves foster care—with the birth family, with another relative, or with an adopted family. Permanency plans also include conditions that families must meet in order for children to

"Reuniting or preventing a child from entering foster care is always our number one goal."[4]

—Jerry Milner, the acting commissioner for the Administration for Children, Youth, and Families

return home. Before a child can return home, birth parents must demonstrate that they can keep the child safe, meet the child's needs, and are prepared to be parents. They may be required to complete parenting or anger management classes, attend counseling, receive drug or alcohol treatment, or show they can provide for a child by getting a steady job and having a safe place to live.

Shrounda Selivanoff worked hard to get her daughter back after she was placed in foster care. She explains the steps she took: "I graduated from a year-long inpatient treatment program, started working full-time and doing all of the services that the court had ordered. Working a job, going to services and working on self is extremely difficult. . . . One by one, I was able to work down the list of required services. I went from non-compliant to partially compliant to compliant."[5] Today, Selivanoff and her daughter are reunited.

How long a child stays in foster care depends on the child's family situation and the availability of foster care in his or her community. Some children only stay in foster care for a short time before returning to their birth family. Others may spend years in the foster care system. Of the more than 250,000 youth who exited

Kinship Care

When children have to be removed from their birth parents, social workers first look for a family member willing and able to take them into their home and provide care. Often, this type of foster placement, called kinship care, offers several advantages for children and their families. First, the children usually already know the adults that will be providing care. Children and birth parents experience less stress and worry if children are placed with someone who is known and trusted by both. In addition, children in kinship care are better able to maintain family connections and relationships. As of September 30, 2016, about 139,000 foster children were placed in the homes of relatives. That is approximately 32 percent of the children in care as of that date, according to the HHS. Sometimes the kinship care arrangement is informal and agreed upon by the parents and relatives. Other times, a local child welfare agency is involved.

foster care during 2016, the median amount of time spent in care was 13.9 months, according to a report by the Child Welfare Information Gateway. If a child remains in foster care for 15 out of 22 months, the law requires a child welfare agency to ask the courts to terminate the birth parents' parental rights and end the legal parent-child relationship. Once parental rights are terminated, the child is available for adoption.

Entering Foster Care

Children enter the foster care system because their families are experiencing a crisis and their birth parents are not able to care for them in a safe and stable home. In 2016 approximately 274,000 children entered the foster care system. The majority of them, 61 percent, were removed because of neglect, according to the ACF, which is part of the HHS. Other common reasons for removal include parental drug abuse (34 percent), a caretaker's inability to cope (14 percent), and physical abuse (12 percent).

Typically, a teacher, neighbor, or family member notices the abuse or neglect and reports it to the police or a child welfare agency. When they receive a report, the police and the child welfare agency investigate the claims. If they decide it is not safe for the child to remain in the home, the child welfare agency goes to court to get temporary custody of the child. If the court approves the agency's request for custody, social workers remove the child from the home. Former foster youth Lisa Marie Basile explains how she entered foster care:

> Both of my parents used drugs for most of my life. I grew up in New Jersey with a hardworking single mother whose vices, at times, were stronger than her resilience. We were living at the poverty level in the port neighborhood of Elizabeth, New Jersey when we lost our apartment and moved in with my sickly grandmother. My mother just sort of let me stop attending school, and this is because she was out dealing with her own issues. A truancy officer must have reported her because shortly after, my brother and I were taken away.[6]

Once a child enters the foster care system, a child welfare agency assigns a caseworker to each foster child. Caseworkers are responsible for keeping the foster child safe and getting him or her into a safe and stable living situation as quickly as possible. Once the child is placed in a foster care arrangement, the caseworker visits regularly to make sure everything is going well and the child's needs are being met. For example, caseworkers make sure foster children are attending school, getting appropriate medical care, and keeping in touch with their birth family.

Increasing Numbers of Youth in Care

According to data released by the ACF, the number of children in foster care is increasing. As of September 2016, more than

437,000 children were in foster care, up from approximately 397,000 children in 2012. These children ranged in age from infants to nineteen-year-olds, with the average age of children in foster care being eight and a half years old as of September 2016.

While the most common cause of a child entering foster care is neglect, drug abuse by one or both parents is increasingly a reason why children land in foster care. In 2016 approximately 92,000 children were removed from their homes and placed in foster care because at least one parent had a drug abuse problem. "The continued trend of parental substance abuse is very concerning, especially when it means children must enter foster care as a result,"[7] says Steven Wagner, the acting assistant secretary for children and families at the ACF.

The growing opioid epidemic across the United States is driving more kids into foster care. "Through my experience as a foster parent, I've seen first-hand how the foster system has been overwhelmed by children removed from homes where the parents are opioid-dependent,"[8] says Troy Quast of the University of South Florida College of Public Health. In a study published in *Health Affairs* in 2018, Quast and his colleagues analyzed the number of children being placed into foster care in Florida and compared it to the number of opioid prescriptions from 2012 to 2015. As the rate of opioid prescriptions increased, they found, so did the rate of children being removed from their homes because of parental neglect. This increase resulted in approximately two thousand additional children being placed into foster care during the period under study.

> "I've seen first-hand how the foster system has been overwhelmed by children removed from homes where the parents are opioid-dependent."[8]
>
> —Troy Quast, a researcher at the University of South Florida College of Public Health

Who Are Foster Parents?

Across the country, foster parents play a critical role in providing temporary care for children who have been removed from their

A foster parent provides a safe, stable home for a child who has had a rough start in life. Some foster parents ultimately adopt their foster children.

homes for a variety of reasons. These people aim to provide a safe and stable home environment for foster children to help them heal from the abuse or neglect they suffered in the past. Foster parents come in all races and ages. They live in cities and rural communities. Many are married (63 percent), but nearly 30 percent are single women according to the Foster Coalition, an advocacy group.

When her two biological adult daughters moved out, single mom Karla Beuchler from Sacramento County, California, says the house felt empty. Over the years, she loved being a mom and the daily parenting tasks like making school lunches and helping with homework. She contacted a local child welfare agency and signed up to become a foster parent. Six years later, Beuchler has fostered two teen girls. She says that she chose to foster teens because she felt that age group had the biggest need. "Most of

The Importance of Siblings

Approximately two-thirds of youth in foster care in America also have a sibling in care. For a variety of reasons, siblings are not always placed with the same family. Even those who are initially placed together are often separated later. This adds to the difficulty young people experience in foster care. Sibling relationships are often the most permanent relationships in a foster child's life. After being removed from their birth parents, relationships with siblings can become even more important. As a result, being separated from siblings in foster care can feel like another loss or punishment to a child. When Mary and her half sister entered foster care, they were together for about a week before being placed in separate families. The separation was difficult for the girls. "I don't think they really took into consideration how separating us would actually have an emotional and psychological effect on both of us, certainly on me," says Mary.

Recognizing the importance of siblings, many child welfare agencies try to find foster families that can keep siblings together. If this is not possible, they recommend that foster families help children continue their relationship with siblings through visits, phone calls, social media, and e-mail. Supporting and strengthening sibling bonds can help foster youth feel more secure and stable.

Quoted in Sarah Farnsworth, "Children Separated from Siblings in Foster Care Feel 'Powerless, Anxious,' CREATE Foundation Study Finds," ABC News (Australia), June 15, 2015. www.abc.net.au.

the kids in foster care are over the age of 8 and little ones get adopted pretty fast," she says. Beuchler encourages others to consider becoming foster parents. "People think it's expensive, but it's not," she says. "Most of the child's care is paid for. You just get to love them."[9]

Some areas of the country are experiencing shortages of foster parents. The shortage of foster parents cannot be explained by a single reason; instead, it is affected by several factors. Some places are experiencing a shortage because of an increase in children coming into the system. In addition, the process of becoming a foster parent can be long and difficult, involving home studies, classes, and background checks before a person is approved. Some potential foster parents feel unprepared to handle children with a variety of behavioral problems or special needs. Some people are also hesitant to become foster parents because they fear becoming too attached to the child and then having to say goodbye when the child returns to his or her birth family or other permanent living situation.

Leaving Foster Care

Foster care is supposed to be a temporary situation until a permanent solution can be found, whether that is returning to live with the birth family or another situation. Every year, a little more than half of the children who leave foster care return to live with their birth parents or a previous caregiver, as the issues that caused them to be removed from their homes have been addressed. Many do not need to return to the foster care system. In 2016 approximately 250,000 children left the foster care system according to ACF. Fifty-one percent returned to live with birth parents or a previous caregiver. Another 7 percent went to live with a relative. Those teens who were eighteen years old were declared emancipated as legal adults and were released from the foster care system.

Although the goal of the foster care system is to reunify children with their birth parents, it is not always possible. In some cases, foster children who cannot return to their parents are adopted by another relative or adult. In 2016 approximately 57,000 foster children were adopted, a slight increase from the 52,000 adopted in 2012. Many were adopted by their foster parents, and others were adopted by an adult relative or a non-relative.

Adopting a foster child can be an uncertain process. The procedures and paperwork required vary from state to state and even county to county. Children are often placed with potential adoptive families and foster parents before they are legally available for adoption and while social workers still explore the possibility of returning them to their birth family. For some, the uncertainty can be emotionally draining. Denise Henderson is a single mom and retired psychologist from Rochester, New York. She remembers the uncertainty she felt while waiting to see whether she would be able to adopt her foster daughter. "My daughter came to live with us as a newborn. It took three long years before the courts freed her for adoption. The weight that lifted off me in that moment was incredible. I didn't realize what a burden I'd been carrying until I no longer had to bear it. Now my daughter is a lovely 13-year-old . . . of whom I couldn't be prouder,"[10] she says.

A Safe Home

A foster family provides a safe and supportive home for youth when their birth families can no longer take care of them. Whether temporary or permanent, foster families are one of the many types of families that make up modern America.

Chapter Two

How I See Myself and My Family

Many youth find it difficult to adjust to life in a foster home. Often, these kids come from environments where they have had little positive feedback or encouragement from their parents and others around them. As they enter foster care, they often have a poor self-image and no real understanding of what a family should be like. Even when leaving a bad situation, foster youth often feel a sense of allegiance to their birth parents and families. Some kids blame themselves for their families being torn apart. These feelings make it difficult for kids to feel good about themselves and develop a real relationship with their foster families.

Yet for some kids, living with a foster family provides the support and stability they need to thrive. For the first time in their lives, these kids are able to develop strong, positive relationships with foster parents and siblings. In a stable home, they learn to trust others, learn to like themselves, and learn what it means to be part of a family. For most of Alexis Griffin's life, her mother struggled with drug addiction while her father was in and out of jail. As a foster teen, Griffin lived in more than ten different homes until she and her sister found stability with their last foster family. "Our last foster parents made the lifetime commitment to be our parents, the ones who we can depend on. We have had our ups and downs like all families do—but . . . they decided to work on being the parents that we need. Even though we had a rough beginning they have made our futures brighter, and for that I am grateful,"[11] she says.

Yet no matter how a foster care experience ends, it almost always begins with a tumultuous jumble of emotions. These include fear, uncertainty, loneliness, anger, and a desperate wish that the situation were different.

Fear and Uncertainty

Entering foster care can be a very scary time for children. Most have been neglected, mistreated, or subjected to unsafe conditions. Some may have lived with parents who are addicted to drugs or who have become too physically sick to care for them. Other children enter the foster care system when a parent dies and no other family member can step in. In these situations, child welfare agencies have little choice but to remove young people from their home.

No matter the circumstances, being separated from a parent or caregiver and placed in foster care can be extremely traumatic and confusing for a child. Often, children are too young to fully understand what is happening to them and the reasons they are being taken from their home. According to the National Child Traumatic Stress Network, some children living in foster care say that the physical act of being removed from their home is the most traumatic part of their separation from their parent or caregiver. In many cases, the child may also be separated from his or her siblings.

These experiences can fill a child with fear and worry. Edgar Carranza entered foster care when he was thirteen years old. Now twenty-three and an advocate for foster kids, he remembers his experience entering foster care: "I was thrown into foster care at age 13 when my father was deported. Up to the day before, I didn't understand what was happening. I couldn't even say good bye to everyone. . . . It was awful."[12]

Being placed in foster care does not necessarily eliminate the uncertainty that comes with being separated from one's parents. Often, children do not stay in one home for their entire time in foster care. Many move from foster home to foster home. Sometimes foster kids move because they have behavioral problems that foster families cannot handle. Others move to a new home because their foster parents are unprepared or unwilling to provide the support and care they need. Regardless of the reason, moving from placement to placement only adds to the uncertainty and the sense of having nothing permanent in their lives.

As a child, Sophia Williams-Baugh lived in eight different foster homes. Moving from place to place, often at a moment's notice, caused significant instability in her life. "When you are forced to live with one person after another, you never know what life has in store for you. You don't know what tomorrow will bring, literally. You can think that all is well and that you have finally found your forever home, then discover that once again you just didn't fit the bill,"[13] she says.

> **"When you are forced to live with one person after another, you never know what life has in store for you. You don't know what tomorrow will bring, literally."[13]**
>
> —Sophia Williams-Baugh, a former foster youth

The Impact of Trauma

Many youth in foster care have experienced significant trauma in their lives, from being abused or neglected to being removed from their families and caregivers. Childhood traumatic stress occurs when youth experience events or situations that interfere with their ability to cope and function in daily life and interact with others. These traumatic experiences disrupt a child's sense of security and safety. It changes how they see themselves and how they see and interact with other people in their lives.

Experiencing trauma at a young age, especially repeated trauma, can cause a child to develop emotional and behavioral problems. Young children may become clingy or regress to younger behaviors such as bed-wetting. Older children may withdraw from others or exhibit aggressive and disruptive behavior. They may be irritable and have angry outbursts and get into fights. Often, they have developed these behaviors as a way to protect themselves from neglect or abuse.

Once placed in foster care, some young people develop strong, positive relationships with their foster parents and siblings. This does not happen in all cases.

Other foster youth develop depression, anxiety, or feelings of guilt. Samantha Smith lived in foster care for several years, frequently moving from one family to another. She struggled with the uncertainty of never knowing how long she would be somewhere and having so little control over her life. She did not know where she belonged or how she fit in:

> Not too many people understand the impact of being taken away from one's biological family and then put in foster care. It's not easy, being introduced to a community of new teachers and friends that you have to get to know, in the face of losing something so important to you. It would be bad enough to be uprooted one time but when you're taken out of that setting suddenly, numerous times, it causes separation anxiety, depression, and many other mental

illnesses. . . . There were times when I'd come home from school and my bags were being packed. I didn't even get to say goodbye to my old friends, and this would happen about every six months or when my foster parents simply didn't want to deal with me anymore.[14]

Being placed with the right foster family, on the other hand, can help young people heal from the trauma they have experienced. Georgette Todd suffered traumas and abuse while living with her drug-using mother and stepfather. After her mother died, Todd entered foster care. Over the next four years, she lived in fourteen different foster homes. At the last placement she finally found the foster mother who was able to help her heal from her past:

It was my last foster mother who saved me from myself. . . . She didn't have any biological children and didn't have these great expectations that I should be perfect. She didn't expect me to open up my loving arms and connect with her right away. No, she only wanted to stabilize my sister and me by creating a solid launching pad for normalcy. She wanted us to focus on finishing high school and prepare for college or a vocational job instead of having us worry where we were going to live day-to-day. . . . She acted like any regular parent would with their child. She made me feel normal.[15]

Feeling Isolated

For many children, entering foster care means being removed from the people and places they have known their whole lives. In an interview with the *Guardian* newspaper, one former foster child talked about the hardships of moving away from one's home and community:

I lost both my parents at the age of 13 and found myself in foster care. The local authority had, and still [has], a short-age of people willing to foster and I found myself moving away from the city where I grew up. This meant I lost my community, my school and also the friends I had known since nursery [school]. Education was a particularly difficult issue as I enrolled in a school where everyone already knew one another. This combined with my inclination to withdraw emotionally on account of my early experiences meant that it was difficult to make new friends.[16]

The experience of being in foster care, surrounded by unfamiliar people, and living in an unfamiliar place can make foster youth feel alone and isolated, as if they have no one to rely on in the entire world. John Devine entered the foster system at age twelve, when his mother died and no family member could take custody of him. "When my social worker explained to me where I was going to live, I felt anxious, and without a doubt, afraid of entering a new environment with people I did not even know," he says. "I remember my first foster mother telling me to not be nervous or scared and to feel like I was part of their family. But did she really understand what emotions I felt, or what thoughts were running through my mind? Did she understand the intensity and how emotionally draining it was to feel like I was an outcast from the rest of the world?" As he moved through four foster homes, Devine felt increasingly isolated and alone. "I started thinking that the only person who could truly understand what I was going through was me. . . . I felt that I was alone in the world, different from everyone else,"[17] he says. Eventually, Devine's social worker suggested that he see a behavioral counselor who helped him work through his feelings of loss and isolation. Today, Devine is pursuing a master's degree in social work and is working with foster youth.

> "I started thinking that the only person who could truly understand what I was going through was me. . . . I felt that I was alone in the world, different from everyone else."[17]
>
> —John Devine, a former foster youth

Encouraging Normalcy

For many youth, childhood is filled with sleepovers, vacations, and milestones like getting a driver's license or landing an after-school job. For foster youth, the law can get in the way of experiencing many of these childhood events. For many years, if a foster youth wanted to sleep over at a friend's house or go to a birthday party, the adults involved had to be fingerprinted and have a background check, which could take weeks to complete. Often, foster children missed out on normal childhood opportunities because foster parents worried they would be held legally liable if something happened to the child. Former foster youth Esther Gross remembers how the foster system's restrictions made it difficult for her to feel like a normal teen and affected her relationships with her foster and birth families:

> When the family went on vacation, I was not allowed to go with them because of foster care agency restrictions. . . . I couldn't go to sleepovers or participate in after-school activities, making it hard for me to make and maintain friendships. . . . These restrictions affected my relationship with my birth family. When my favorite uncle passed away, I wasn't allowed to attend his funeral. The restrictions were a constant reminder that I didn't belong—I wasn't a full member of my birth family or my foster family.

In recent years, some states have recognized that restrictions intended to protect children actually add to their isolation. These states have loosened certain restrictions to encourage more normalcy for foster youth.

Esther Gross, "Why Normalcy Is Important for Youth in Foster Care," Child Trends, May 18, 2016. www.childtrends.org.

Even the smallest things can magnify the feeling of being alone and different from other people. For example, when asked to make a family tree for school, foster children might not have any pictures of their birth family or even of themselves. Other times, foster youth may feel self-conscious when they are unable to afford the latest clothing trends and toys and instead have to wear secondhand clothing or use donated school supplies.

Building a Wall

The uncertainty and isolation that many foster youth experience can cause them to put up a tough exterior to keep those around them at a distance. They use this barrier to protect themselves from more hurt and rejection. If they never bond with a new foster family, they believe, they will not get hurt when they are eventually moved to another placement or the adults in their lives disappoint them again. As foster youth Breanna explains, "Trust is something you have to earn and I have learned that it's very hard to trust people. It takes me a while to actually get to the point of trusting people."[18]

Many foster youth feel lonely and isolated after being removed from their birth parents. Feeling accepted and making new friends can be challenging for them.

Aria Williams entered the foster care system at age eight. She spent several years moving from home to home before she landed with her current foster family at age fourteen. Although she wanted to belong to a family, Williams found it difficult to trust adults and frequently acted out in anger. "Looking back now I realize that I was not very nice to my foster parents or my caseworkers. Being in foster care forced me to build a wall inside of myself that helped me block my emotions from others and push people who cared about me away. But beneath it all, I longed for a family," she says. Eventually, Williams met the foster parents who would help her break down her emotional wall:

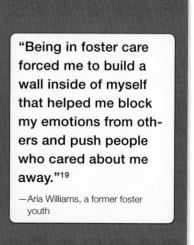

"Being in foster care forced me to build a wall inside of myself that helped me block my emotions from others and push people who cared about me away."[19]

—Aria Williams, a former foster youth

My [foster] parents helped me by allowing me to express myself without judgement and loving me for who I was. They saw the potential in me that I could never see myself. They realized my past was hard, and they gave me the space and support I needed. My parents would always tell me they loved me and give me lots of hugs. I really needed affection, so hugs and kind words helped me to open up to them. It took time, but slowly the walls I had built were torn down.[19]

At age sixteen, Williams's foster parents adopted her, creating her long-desired forever family.

Guilt and Blame

Many youth in foster care blame themselves and feel guilty about having been removed from their birth parents. Some wish they could return to their birth parents despite the abuse or neglect.

Preserving Cultural Identity

Foster families and foster youth come in every race, religion, ethnicity, and sexual orientation. When a child enters foster care, he or she may be placed in a foster family of a different race, culture, or religion. When this occurs, it can be difficult for a child to maintain a sense of his or her cultural identity. Edgar is a Hispanic youth who has spent time in foster care. Before foster care, he remembers his stepmother making traditional Hispanic foods such as flautas, guacamole, and beans. When he entered foster care, Edgar experienced a culture shock. He lived with non-Hispanic families and was introduced to more American foods and culture. During his time in various foster families, Edgar also lost touch with some Hispanic traditions and had trouble staying in touch with his birth family. Determined not to lose his cultural identity, today Edgar lives in his own apartment and works on re-creating his stepmother's traditional recipes in his own kitchen. He also practices his Spanish, listens to Hispanic music, and keeps in touch with his brother, father, and cousins.

Children's Rights, a group that advocates for children in foster care, is working to help foster youth like Edgar preserve their cultural identity. They have lobbied for more frequent visitation between foster youth and birth parents. In addition, reforms in several states have resulted in youth being placed in foster homes closer to their schools and communities and more sibling groups being placed together. They hope these steps and others will help youth maintain their cultural identity while living in foster families.

These feelings of guilt can make it even more difficult to attach to a foster family. By bonding with foster parents, children may feel as if they are somehow betraying their birth family. Former foster youth Lisa Marie Basile remembers finding it difficult to bond with her foster family because she still wanted to be with her birth mother. "The couple who became my foster parents for my high school years gave me a good home and access to an incredible school system, but I still would rather have been with my mother. Unlike my foster parents, she understood me on a deep level,"[20] she says.

These feelings of guilt and blame can make it difficult to navigate relationships between foster families and birth families. Young people who are experiencing painful feelings can lash out at those around them or withdraw from others. "We don't recognize how they're grieving," says Patricia Bresee, a former juvenile court judge. "We should all think about what it would mean to lose a parent. They're your rock. Even if the rock is a crag that's cutting our hand, it's still the only rock we've ever known."[21] However, having regular contact with birth parents can help kids and teens work through and express their feelings, which makes them less likely to take out these feelings on others. It can also help them develop a positive relationship with their foster family.

Chapter Three

How Others See Me and My Family

Foster youth and their families are often viewed by others through the lenses of judgment, stereotypes, and myths. How others view them can affect young people living in care, often in a negative way. As Margie Fink, a foster parent, explains,

> People are often hesitant to be near these children. As their caregivers, people may be quick to praise us and equally as quick to drop us as friends. . . . I was experiencing a very rough week as a foster parent. Events were taking place that led me to feel as if one of our kids was being labeled and judged. It all came to a head when I saw my child walk over to talk to another child and then saw my child get pushed away from the other child by their parent.[22]

Fink's experience with the other parent illustrates how a negative view of foster care can affect how others see and interact with foster youth.

The Stigma of Foster Care

Young people living with foster families enter the system because of circumstances beyond their control. Yet these young people are often viewed—mistakenly—as delinquents, as dangerous, and as damaged goods. The stigma attached to foster care is no small problem. Nearly half of Americans believe that youth land in foster care because of something they themselves have done. According to the 2017 US Adoption Attitudes Survey prepared for the Dave

Thomas Foundation, a nonprofit dedicated to finding permanent homes for foster children, nearly half (46 percent) of people surveyed said they believe (either strongly or somewhat) that young people in foster care are there because they are juvenile delinquents. And this attitude often transfers from adults to kids. "Some kids felt the need to steer clear of us," says a nineteen-year-old former foster youth. "Kids think we're some kind of crazy psychos, that something went wrong with us because we live shattered lives."[23]

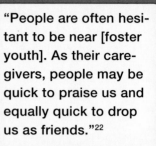

"People are often hesitant to be near [foster youth]. As their caregivers, people may be quick to praise us and equally quick to drop us as friends."[22]

—Foster parent Margie Fink

In reality, most foster kids enter the system because they have been abused or neglected by the adults who are responsible for caring for them. "It's not our fault that we were put in this situation in which we don't live with our parents or have a mom and dad we can talk to and who will be there no matter what. Society doesn't seem to understand that we are not to be labeled, we are not a statistic on the map, failure is not fixed into our destiny. Society doesn't seem to understand that we are people, too,"[24] writes one person who lived in foster care as a child.

Many people also see foster kids as dangerously aggressive. They hear stories about foster kids hurting people, biting, kicking, and getting into fights. Some people avoid children in foster care and their families because they believe the foster youth are dangerous. "I've lost count of the times teachers and parents of other kids formed fears or prejudices of a child, predicated on a perennial assumption that they had done something pretty terrible to wind up in care,"[25] writes Amma Mante, who has worked with kids and teens in foster care.

As Fink explains, young people who live with these labels sometimes begin to believe they must be true:

Two of our children came to our home with preconceived notions of who they were: one was "stupid" and one was "bad." In an everyday conversation it even came up that

27

one of the children thought it was his fault that the kids were removed from their biological home. As foster and adoptive parents, we often have our work cut out for us as we try to erase these self (or other) imposed labels from our kiddos.[26]

The US Adoption Attitudes Survey also found that people commonly believe that foster youth have problems with trust and bonding (45 percent), behavioral problems (40 percent), problems in school and learning (33 percent), and problems with physical health and disability (22 percent). To some extent, these beliefs are true. Trauma experienced in childhood can trigger bad behavior and other defense mechanisms that help keep people at a distance.

Foster youth say they are often viewed by others as troublemakers. Labels and judgments that are based on stereotypes make it hard for young people to adjust to new settings.

Experts say these behaviors are a means of protection from future hurt and disappointment. Some young people have experienced so much upheaval in their lives, they do not fully understand how to behave in a normal environment. "They're not bad kids; they're kids who are reacting in a very normal way, the way any of us would if everything we knew today were different tomorrow—your mom is gone, your dad is gone . . . everything you once knew is gone. We would be suffering grief and loss, too,"[27] explains Ramona Denby-Brinson, a professor in the School of Social Work at the University of Nevada, Las Vegas. With proper guidance, understanding, and counseling, youth living in foster care can lead full and productive lives.

> "They're not bad kids; they're kids who are reacting in a very normal way, the way any of us would if everything we knew today were different tomorrow—your mom is gone, your dad is gone . . . everything you once knew is gone."[27]
>
> —Ramona Denby-Brinson, a professor in the School of Social Work at the University of Nevada, Las Vegas

Hiding a Secret

Because of the stigma attached to foster care, many youth living in foster families are reluctant to tell anyone about their family situation. Going to school and living in communities filled with kids who live with their parents can make youth feel self-conscious and different than their peers. Many choose to hide the fact that they are living in a foster family. One youth who has spent time in the foster care system explains, "As a foster youth I often struggle internally with the decision to reveal my foster status and at which point to do so. I wonder how the person will react, will they treat me differently now that they know this about me, and how do I explain myself afterwards?"[28]

For those who choose to hide their status, there is constant worry of being found out and exposed. One former foster youth remembers the time his teacher outed him in front of his classmates. He was on the football team and none of his friends and teammates knew that he was in the foster care system. With his secret in the open, he felt embarrassed and humiliated.

Brianna, a teen who was adopted from foster care, says that talking about being in the foster care system can be very difficult. "You just never know if someone will laugh at you or treat you differently or just simply try to understand," she says. By hiding this part of their lives, foster youth can avoid difficult conversations and embarrassment. "Being in the system is harder to talk about for the simple fact that everyone knows that something bad happened to you or your parents to even be put in the system. It is not easy talking about it because you always get the question 'So why are you in foster care?' And honestly," says Brianna, "that is not something people like to talk about just out of the blue."[29]

Answering Difficult Questions

"What happened to your parents?" Many foster youth dread questions like that. They understand that other kids might just be curious about a foster kid's life because their circumstances are so different from their own. Knowing that does not make these questions easier to answer. It is extremely difficult to explain to others that they are in foster care because their parents are drug addicts or abused them or that they do not know how long they will be living with their current foster family. As a former foster youth, Brianna explains that "many people think that it's just okay to go up to someone and ask them about their biological parents, but in all honesty it is not okay at all. It's hard. People ask you thirty million questions. Who's your mom? Where's your dad? Those are your parents? Your parents are *white*? These are just a few [questions that] people get."[30]

> "Many people think that it's just okay to go up to someone and ask them about their biological parents, but in all honesty it is not okay at all. It's hard."[30]
>
> —Brianna, a teen adopted from foster care

Foster Parent Stereotypes

Foster kids are not the only ones who are stereotyped. Foster parents are often described stereotypically as being mean, uncaring, and money-grubbers. One common stereotype is that foster parents do what they do for the money. In truth, although foster parents do receive a stipend to cover a foster child's basic living expenses, this money rarely covers the cost of providing for the child, let alone being an income source. And although some foster parents should not be foster parents, many take kids into their homes because they believe they can help a child in need.

Media portrayals often reinforce negative stereotypes. In a 2016 episode of the television show *What Would You Do?* actors played the roles of a foster mother, her foster son, and her biological daughter. The three were seated in a crowded diner. The foster mom loudly told her foster son that taking care of him was a job and that if she adopted him, she would lose money. Unsuspecting diner customers who overheard the actors' conversation scolded the foster mom.

Real foster parents say the segment reinforces negative stereotypes. Richard Heyl de Ortiz, the executive director of the Adoptive and Foster Family Coalition, explains how media portrayals like this can affect how people see foster families. "This coming school year, as teachers who saw this review their class rosters and see that one of the children in their class is in foster care, you can bet they will eye the foster parents suspiciously, at least initially. That's the type of damage this piece does."

Richard Heyl de Ortiz, "Perpetuating Foster Parent Stereotypes," Adoptive and Foster Family Coalition, July 22, 2016. http://affcny.org.

Sometimes, youth simply want to put a difficult past and painful emotions behind them. Having to answer prying questions about their past makes it very difficult to move forward in rebuilding their lives. "Being asked these questions can sometimes hurt someone's feelings or make them silent. It's not that we don't want to tell you, it's simply that we want to put the past behind us. I just tell people that I have my family and that's all I need. It takes a lot for someone to open up about just being adopted or in the system,"[31] says Brianna.

How the Mainstream Media Portray Foster Families

Many people know very little about the foster care system and what it is like to live in a foster family. Often, the information that they do have comes from the mainstream media. Over the years, the media have perpetuated several foster care stereotypes. News stories about foster care often present it in a negative light, focusing on stories about abusive foster parents or disruptive foster kids. News features spotlight the poor outcomes with youth in foster care, the problems they have bonding and forming relationships, and the difficulties these young people face as they transition to adulthood. Michelle Burnette has fostered more than forty children and agrees that the news media often present a negative view of foster care. She explains, "I think all too often the focus is on the negative and not on the good things that happen, the kids that were reunited with their family or the adoption."[32]

On television and in film, the portrayal of youth and their foster families is often based on stereotypes. Kids and teens living in foster care are often shown as poor, disadvantaged, and struggling to survive while they are forced to live with cruel and uncaring caregivers, such as in the movie *Annie*. On television, movies that tackle foster care frequently present stereotypes of drug-addicted birth parents, cruel foster parents, and delinquent foster youth. "To be fair, I cringe every time I hear about a foster care project. Hollywood rarely gets it right when it comes to foster care. Occasionally they will get close, with embellishments. Most of the time they miss the mark completely,"[33] says Chris Chimielewski, the editor of *Foster Focus* magazine and a former foster youth.

"I believe the accurate representation of foster youth in the media is necessary to destroy the negative stigma most people have about foster care and empower more people to get involved in supporting foster children."[34]

—Shalita O'Neale, the founder and executive director of Hope Forward, Inc.

Television shows are increasingly portraying foster families, including those headed by lesbian and gay couples, in a realistic and positive light. Such depictions help to break down negative stereotypes.

Those involved in the foster care system believe that accurate representation of youth in foster care and their families would help break down negative stereotypes. "I believe the accurate representation of foster youth in the media is necessary to destroy the negative stigma most people have about foster care and empower more people to get involved in supporting foster children or, in the very least, inspire people to educate themselves about the foster care system and how and why it exists,"[34] says Shalita O'Neale, the founder and executive director of Hope Forward, Inc., a non-profit organization that works with youth in the foster care system.

In recent years, portrayals of foster care in the media have been praised for examining real-life issues that impact foster families and presenting a more realistic picture of what life is like for these families. On the Freeform cable network, *The Fosters* was a television drama that followed the lives of a multicultural foster family headed by a lesbian couple. When developing the show, its creators reached out to people in the foster care system to help them present foster care in a realistic way. The show tackled issues such as abuse by foster parents and the complicated feelings kids in foster families can have for their biological parents. Jamie Smith, an eighteen-year-old youth living in foster care says that for the most part, the show was a realistic depiction of life in a foster family. She appreciates how the show handled the conflicted feeling the kids had about their birth parents as well as how it feels to arrive at a strange house. Smith explains that the show highlighted the important reality "that it's okay to be in foster care, and it's okay to be foster parents."[35]

Changing Perceptions

In recent years, there has been a positive shift in how people see foster families. While there are still some people who view children in foster care in a negative light, more are becoming accepting of these children and their families. Dr. Kalyani Gopal, the clinical

Fighting Stereotypes Together

Recognizing the harm that stereotypes can cause, a nonprofit organization called Together We Rise is working to change negative stereotypes and improve life for youth in foster care. The organization provides resources such as school supplies, bicycles, and scholarships. It also created a program that shares happy pictures of foster children on their adoption day on social media. These adoption-day photos celebrate a foster child's adoption and give the public a real-life view of youth and the people who take care of them. In each photo, the child stands next to signs that reveal how much time they spent in foster care. The organization hopes that sharing happy success stories from foster care will help break down stereotypes and remind people that foster youth are simply children who deserve joy and are part of happy families across the country.

director at Mid America Psychological and Counseling Services, says that "less often than not, I talk to families who have come into contact with foster children and invite them over to play and engage with their children and extended families. . . . More and more American families are inclined to include foster children in their communities."[36]

Gopal attributes these changing attitudes to positive attention on foster families in the media through shows like *The Fosters* and stories of celebrities like Angelina Jolie and Sandra Bullock welcoming children into their families through foster care and adoption. "There is a growing awareness of inclusive acceptance rather than exclusive fear,"[37] she says. Gopal remains optimistic that further steps can be made to reduce negative stereotypes of foster families. Through positive examples, success stories, and improvements in the training of foster families, the way people view foster youth can continue to change in a positive way.

Not Just a Foster Kid

Youth living in foster care are already dealing with a number of challenges, including how people see them. They do not want to be defined as a *foster kid* with all the stereotypes attached. Instead, they want people to see them as normal young people, with the same hopes and challenges as their peers, who happen to live in a foster family. Barbara, a teen living in foster care, explains, "We're people. We're no different than anyone but we've been through a lot. The things that happen to us, we didn't ask for. But we wake up and try just like you—it's everyday things that make us just like you."[38]

Chapter Four

Other People Who Have Families Like Mine

Many well-known, successful people have been part of a foster family at some time during their lives. Among them are football player Jimmy Graham, actress Tiffany Haddish, and country musician Jimmy Wayne. All three faced challenges related to living in foster care—and all three overcame the obstacles and went on to become successful adults.

Abandoned in a Stairwell

A five-time Pro Bowl tight end in the National Football League (NFL), Jimmy Graham has been open about his time in the foster care system as a youth. Born on November 24, 1986, to a young single mother, Graham spent his early childhood in Goldsboro, North Carolina. Graham's mother often struggled to make ends meet and frequently left the young boy with family members. Eventually she made a custody agreement that assigned her ex-husband as his guardian. However, the ex-husband wanted a monthly payment of ninety-eight dollars from Graham's mother, which she was not willing to pay. Instead, she dropped off nine-year-old Graham in the stairwell of a social services agency.

Although Graham's mother ultimately agreed to bring him back home, it did not last for long. One morning when he was eleven, Graham's mother told him they were going for a ride. The ride quickly turned into a nightmare. "She stopped the car and told me to get out, I had no idea what was going on," Graham remembers. She had driven to a group home for orphans and troubled youth and, then and there, she signed custody of the boy over to the state. Graham was led into his new home. "She just left me there," says Graham. "I was small and scared. My mom had left me in a kid jail, basically."[39]

In the group home, Graham found himself living with older boys, many of whom had troubled pasts. "There were violent offenders, thieves and deviants. I was NOT supposed to be there. I was a normal, polite kid I had to figure out how to get along there,"[40] he says. He was bullied and beaten repeatedly by the older boys; one time, the beating was so bad that he spent three days recovering in bed. Graham called his mother many times, begging her to let him come home, but she refused.

Finding the Support to Succeed

After nine months at the group home, Graham's mother relented and brought him home. However, the new boyfriend in her life beat and abused him. To escape, Graham began to visit a weekly prayer group that offered free food. At the prayer group, he met Becky Vinson, a church youth counselor and young single mother. Over a few months, Graham and Vinson formed a bond. He talked with her about his problems at home and his fear of being sent back to the group home. Graham often spent evenings at Vinson's home, having dinner and staying as late as he could.

When Vinson saw Graham's failing report card during his freshman year of high school, she sat him down and told him that he had a lot of potential and pushed him to do better. And then Vinson made sure that Graham studied and did his homework. She realized that Graham needed a family that wanted him and became his foster parent. Although she was not rich, Vinson gave Graham the stability and support that he craved. She talked to Graham's mother and eventually became his legal guardian.

Although the little family struggled to pay the bills at times, Graham finally felt like he had a family with Vinson and her daughter. Slowly, with Vinson's support, Graham's grades improved to As and Bs. He also began to take sports more seriously, becoming an important member of his high school basketball team. Eventually,

After being abandoned by his birth mother more than once, professional tight end Jimmy Graham finally found support and stability with a young single mother who eventually became his legal guardian.

he earned a basketball scholarship to play at the University of Miami in Florida. A talented basketball player, Graham played for the Miami Hurricanes from 2005 to 2009. He graduated in May 2009 with a double major in marketing and management.

During Graham's junior year, Bernie Kosar, a former NFL quarterback and University of Miami alumnus, encouraged Graham to play football. After some coaching and training with Kosar, Graham stayed at the school after graduation to take a few graduate classes and play a season of football. He played as a tight end for Miami and finished the season with seventeen receptions for 213 yards and five touchdowns. His play on the field caught the eye of several NFL scouts.

At the 2010 NFL draft, Graham was selected by the New Orleans Saints. In his first year as a starter in 2011, Graham set and tied many Saints records and was selected for his first Pro Bowl. The Saints players also voted Graham as the 2011 winner of the team's Ed Block Courage Award, which recognizes players who overcome adversity. In 2018, the now thirty-one-year-old Graham is a nine-season NFL veteran and one of the top tight ends in the league. Since entering the NFL in 2010, he has accumulated sixty-eight hundred receiving yards and fifty-nine touchdowns. Graham attributes his early challenges with making him the strong person that he is today. He explains,

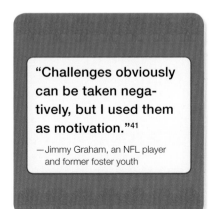

"Challenges obviously can be taken negatively, but I used them as motivation."[41]

—Jimmy Graham, an NFL player and former foster youth

As a young kid, I was shown my worth by everyone older than me, including my parents. But I never lost belief in myself and in my future. Those moments strengthened me. Challenges obviously can be taken negatively, but I used them as motivation. When someone tells you you're not going to be anything or you're not good enough, that's motivation for me to prove them wrong and strive for something better. To work hard in school and try and get a scholarship. I took on each and every mountain in my life with that same attitude . . . of going at this as hard as I can to prove everyone who said I couldn't do it wrong.[41]

Laughing Through Pain

Actress and comedian Tiffany Haddish spent several years as a teen in foster homes. She was born on December 3, 1979, in Los Angeles to a father who was from Eritrea, Africa, and an American mother. When she was very young, Haddish's father left the family. Her mother remarried and had four more children. When

The Felix Organization

For more than a decade, Darryl "DMC" McDaniels, from the hip-hop group Run-DMC, has been helping youth in foster care. A former foster child himself, McDaniels founded the Felix Organization in 2006 with Emmy-winning casting director Sheila Jaffe, who had also spent time in foster care. The Felix Organization works to enrich the lives of children growing up in the foster care system. Its signature programs are Camp Felix, a summer camp in Upstate New York, and Camp Felix West, a camp in Los Angeles, which are specifically designed for foster youth. Throughout the year the Felix Organization also sponsors programs to give foster youth positive experiences and opportunities that will help them become successful young adults. "Sheila and I had a dream . . . years ago. And now we are amazed and humbled how that dream has turned into a reality. I want these kids to understand that there is no one more special than them in this world," says McDaniels.

Quoted in Look to the Stars, "The Felix Organization Celebrates 11 Years with Dance This Way Benefit," April 21, 2017. www.looktothestars.org.

Haddish was eight, her mother was in a serious car accident and suffered a traumatic brain injury. After three months in the hospital, her mother returned home with a very different personality, becoming mean, abusive, and volatile. "I swore she had a demon in her. It's so scary,"[42] remembers Haddish. As the oldest child, Haddish stepped in to take care of her younger siblings. Even at her young age, Haddish learned to use comedy to cope with her mother after the accident:

> I was with her for a few years before we got taken away from her, so that's where I feel like I really developed my comedy chops because I figured if I make her laugh, you know, she won't hit me. You know, when you have a brain injury it's very hard, and especially if before the injury you

were a very intellectual, intelligent person that has an excellent vocabulary, and then you can't pull your words anymore and you get frustrated. And she would hit and stuff, and like I would just try to—if I could make her laugh then I probably won't get hit. But I'm grateful for the experience though. You know, like, I've built a whole career off of being funny, trying to, you know, keep from getting punched.[43]

Eventually, doctors diagnosed Haddish's mother with schizophrenia. When Haddish was thirteen, her mother could no longer take care of her children. Haddish and her siblings were removed from the home and placed in foster care. For two years she bounced among group homes and foster families. She remembers having a hard time fitting in at her new middle school. When Haddish was fifteen, her grandmother gained custody of her and her siblings through the foster care system.

Although cracking jokes helped Haddish cope with her turmoil at home, it also got her into trouble at school. Her social worker sat her down and gave her a choice: she could see a psychiatric therapist or go to comedy camp. Haddish chose the comedy camp, where she worked with several celebrities, including Richard Pryor and Dane Cook. The experience gave her the confidence to believe that she was smart and talented and launched her interest in a career in comedy.

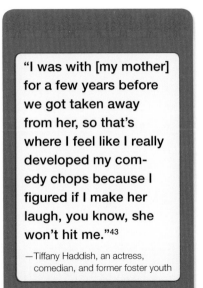

"I was with [my mother] for a few years before we got taken away from her, so that's where I feel like I really developed my comedy chops because I figured if I make her laugh, you know, she won't hit me."[43]

—Tiffany Haddish, an actress, comedian, and former foster youth

After graduating from high school, Haddish struck out on her own to pursue her career. At times, money was so tight that she lived in her car. In 2006 she got her first break as a contestant on the *Who's Got Jokes?* comedy competition television show. From there, she appeared in supporting roles in several television sitcoms and comedy films. Her breakout role came in 2017, when she starred as part of an ensemble cast in the movie *Girls Trip*, along with Regina Hall, Queen Latifah, and Jada Pinkett Smith. Haddish's performance earned high praise and a prestigious best supporting actress award from the New York Film Critics Circle in January 2018. In 2017 she also became the first female African American comedian to host *Saturday Night Live*. In 2018 Haddish costarred with fellow comedian Tracy Morgan in a new television sitcom, *The Last O.G.*

Throughout her career, Haddish has not forgotten her time in foster care. In 2018 the actress donated the proceeds from VIP ticket sales to two sold-out Atlantic City casino shows to the Court Appointed Special Advocates, a nonprofit organization that provides court advocates for kids in foster care. The money will be used to buy youth in the foster care system new suitcases. When former foster care kids describe their moves in and out of different homes, many say that the few possessions they have are often stuffed into a plastic trash bag. Katy Gibson entered foster care at age two but moved in and out of various homes throughout her childhood. When she packed her belongings, she recalls, her "suitcase" was a trash bag. "There is nothing more degrading and belittling than having to shove your belongings into a big black trash bag!" she writes. "As a foster care child, there is not a lot that is actually yours. . . . Shoving the things you love most, into something intended for trash, makes you feel lower than dirt."[44] Haddish remembers this well, which is why she asked that her donation be used to buy suitcases for kids.

Discovering a Love of Music

Award-winning country musician Jimmy Wayne spent time living in foster care and today uses his songs and life story to increase public awareness about foster care. Wayne had a chaotic childhood. He was born in 1972 in Kings Mountain, North Carolina. His dad was not around, and his mother had bipolar disorder and used drugs. Random strangers came and went in and out

Country singer Jimmy Wayne says he got his first view of a healthy family when he was placed in foster care, but then he was returned to his birth mother and a very unstable home life.

of the home, often drinking, doing drugs, and getting into fights. Many times, Wayne and his older sister went hungry because there was not enough food. When he was nine, Wayne's mother was admitted to a psychiatric facility, and Wayne and his sister were sent to a home for children awaiting placement with a foster family. Thirty days later they had been placed with a family. "For the first time I saw what a healthy family looked like. They were loving. They were consistent. They took me to baseball games and gave me cookies and milk before bed. When the social worker told us six months later that our mom was out of the hospital and wanted us back, I cried. I loved Mom, but I knew what was waiting for us at home: chaos, filth, hunger and worse,"[45] says Wayne.

From the ages of nine to sixteen, Wayne drifted in and out of foster care. "I went to 12 schools in two years. I learned not to get attached to anyone. What's the use of getting close to people if you're just going to have to leave them or they're going to leave you, sometimes without even getting to say goodbye?"[46] he says.

At age sixteen, Wayne was on his own and homeless. He slept on friends' couches or outside and took odd jobs to earn money for food. One day he stopped at an elderly couple's woodshop and asked for work. The woman, Bea Costner, agreed to let him mow their lawn once a week. After six weeks, she offered him a place to sleep in their spare bedroom. "I stayed for the next six years. Russell Costner passed away from cancer several months after I moved in, and Bea became like a mother to me. She was the sweetest person I'd ever met, and the structure she provided gave me a sense of safety. I gradually began to trust that with her, I had found a real home,"[47] says Wayne.

> "Bea became like a mother to me. She was the sweetest person I'd ever met, and the structure she provided gave me a sense of safety. I gradually began to trust that with her, I had found a real home."[47]
>
> —Jimmy Wayne, a country music singer and songwriter

With a growing sense of security, Wayne discovered his love of music, playing guitar and singing in a band. After he graduated from high school in 1992, he earned a degree in criminal justice. At the same time, he pursued his passion for music. In 2003 he released his first album, which generated hits such as "Stay Gone" and "I Love You This Much," which both reached the top ten on the Billboard country music charts. His hit single "Do You Believe Me Now," earned the millionaire award for reaching 1 million radio spins. Wayne has toured with country superstar Brad Paisley and has performed at the Grand Ole Opry in Nashville hundreds of times.

In 2010 Wayne walked from Nashville to Phoenix to raise awareness for kids in the foster care system. He has written a best-selling memoir of his life and time in foster care. In 2017 he announced the launch of a new record label called Bea Hive

Voices for the Voiceless

In October 2017, Broadway stars and celebrities took to the stage for the third annual Voices for the Voiceless benefit in New York City. The concert featured performances and special appearances by two-time Tony nominee Jonathan Groff, *Glee*'s Jenna Ushkowitz, four-time Tony-winning producer Jeffrey Seller, and *Orange Is the New Black*'s Danielle Brooks, and more. They sang, danced, and raised awareness for the issues faced by foster youth. At 2016's concert, actress Rosie Perez, who was adopted out of foster care, shared her story and told how she prayed each night as a child to find a forever home. Proceeds from the event benefit You Gotta Believe, a New York–based nonprofit organization that focuses on finding permanent families for youth in foster care aged thirteen and older. Over three years, the annual event raised more than $1 million.

Records, named after his foster mom Bea Costner. Today Wayne continues to raise awareness about foster care by performing, writing books, and speaking at events.

Building a Hopeful Future

Many people who have spent time living with a foster family have gone on to be successful, productive adults. Finding a support system—relatives, foster parents, or other trusted adults—is an important part of helping foster youth feel secure enough to pursue and discover their talents and passions.

Chapter Five

When Foster Care and Family Ties End

After leaving foster care in his late teens, Devontae Pearson struggled to make it on his own. After foster care ended, he lacked the support of a traditional family. At one point, he was homeless. "It was horrible," Pearson says. "I never took a liking to living in the streets."[48] Today, twenty-four-year-old Pearson has found the support he needs to help him reach his goals. He is attending a local community college while also working in a carpentry apprenticeship through YouthBuild Louisville, a Kentucky program that helps young adults learn a building trade. Through the apprenticeship, Pearson has discovered his interest in building and hopes to pursue a career in carpentry. YouthBuild also helped Pearson find a new apartment, part of a complex designed to house young adults who have aged out of the foster care system at eighteen but still need support and housing while they continue their education. The apartment complex is sponsored by Family Scholar House, a Louisville nonprofit organization that offers support for single parents and young adults who have been in foster care.

Lynn Rippy, the executive director of YouthBuild Louisville, says the program for former foster youth is needed to help young adults who lack family support. "Most of us have somebody in our lives to talk to, to keep us moving," Rippy says. "It's just not true for many kids right now." Many teens who leave the foster care system at age eighteen want to be independent, but discover they need help. "Maybe one out of 100 are able to pull themselves up by their bootstraps, but maybe they had a bootstrap," Rippy says. "If we want these young people to be productive, we have to offer them the kind of physical and emotional support they need to become self-sufficient."[49]

Leaving Foster Care

Like Pearson, many youth leave the foster care system at age eighteen. At that age, they are considered adults who are old enough to be responsible for taking care of themselves. If they are living with a foster family, the formal foster care arrangement officially ends.

When youth age out of the foster care system, state funding that helped pay for housing, medical, and other expenses is no longer available to them. They also no longer have caseworkers to talk to about problems they encounter. Many go from having resources and people supporting them to being alone in the world.

For some foster youth who have established a bond with foster families, the relationship with their foster parents and siblings continues even after a formal foster care arrangement ends. Former foster youth David Foster explains,

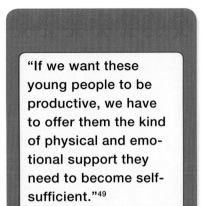

"If we want these young people to be productive, we have to offer them the kind of physical and emotional support they need to become self-sufficient."[49]

—Lynn Rippy, the executive director of YouthBuild Louisville

> I was lucky—I could have left at 16 but stayed with my foster carers until 18 when I left for college. I am now 49 and they are in their seventies—they, over time, with trust and patience became my parents. . . . They stuck with me—and even in my twenties when the emotional issues I was dealing with became too much, they were there. . . . I have no idea who, what or where I would be if I had not struck gold by having these amazing people care for me.[50]

Unfortunately, many teens leaving foster care lack this support. Although the primary goal of the foster care system is to reunite youth with their birth families or find a permanent home for them through adoption, it does not always happen. In 2016 more than seventeen thousand young adults aged out of foster care at age eighteen without being reunited with their families or being adopted, according to the HHS. During their time in the foster care system, these youth often live in multiple homes and attend multiple schools. This transiency makes it difficult for them to develop the long-lasting, permanent relationships they need for support after they leave the foster care system. "There is a difference in the support system for kids aging out of foster [care] than the kid who is in a typical family,"[51] says Jill Marano, the assistant director of the Department of Family Services in Clark County, Nevada.

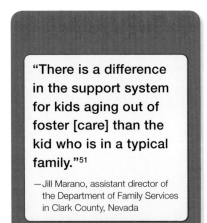

"There is a difference in the support system for kids aging out of foster [care] than the kid who is in a typical family."[51]

—Jill Marano, assistant director of the Department of Family Services in Clark County, Nevada

When she turned eighteen, LaTasha C. Watts aged out of the foster care system and was responsible for taking care of herself. Suddenly, she had to find a place to live and get a job, all without the support of a family. She explains that

the scariest part about being in foster care for me was turning 18. The average kid cannot wait to turn eighteen, graduate from high school and get ready for their journey to college or to travel down that brave road to adulthood. However, by the time I turned 18, the road to college was a distant memory. Instead I was constantly looking for a place to live, couch surfing, trying to figure out how to pay for my most basic needs—on some days I even had to figure out how I was going to eat (and believe you me, there were plenty of nights that I went to bed hungry).[52]

Through the YouthBuild program, a young man learns how to make improvements to a roof overhang. This program teaches job skills and assists young adults who have aged out of the foster care system.

Lacking Basic Skills and Support

When youth age out of the foster care system, they are expected to take on a number of adult responsibilities, such as finding a place to live, finding a job, pursuing higher education, opening a bank account, budgeting their money, taking care of health needs, and more. While tackling these responsibilities, many foster youth lack the social, emotional, and financial support that a family provides to other young adults. "Young people like me who age out of the system usually don't have the luxury of having a family to help," says former foster youth Shantel. "The decisions we face every day—how we pay our bills, put food in our mouths and keep a roof over our heads—are difficult, and we have to answer them without the guidance or support of a family."[53]

Covenant House

Approximately 20 percent of youth who age out of foster care at age eighteen become homeless. One nonprofit trying to change this statistic is Covenant House, with locations in thirty-one cities in six countries. Covenant House offers homeless youth a safe place to stay and develop the life skills they need to live independently. More than one-third of the young people who get help at Covenant House were formerly in foster care. At Covenant House, they find more than just shelter, clean clothes, and a hot meal. The organization also offers education services to help them earn their GEDs as well as certifications for professions ranging from culinary to medical. The organization also helps young adults find jobs and get counseling.

Randall spent several years in foster care before being adopted. When he turned eighteen, however, his adoptive mother threw him out of the house because the subsidy checks she received for him stopped. He was homeless until he found Covenant House in Philadelphia. He lived there for two years while the organization helped him find a job and learn the skills he needed to live independently. Today Randall is employed full-time, lives in his own apartment, and has been admitted to a college.

Many teens leaving foster care also lack the basic skills needed to successfully live independently. During their time in foster care, many have lived under strict rules that do not give them the opportunity to gain the life experiences that will help them live independently. According to a 2017 report by the Department of Children and Family Services in Louisiana, many foster youth live in homes where they are not allowed in the kitchen, not allowed to use the washer and dryer, rely on others to wake them up, and have people driving them where they need to go. As a result, many of these young people do not learn how to make the daily decisions and perform the basic tasks of living independently.

Teens who age out of the foster care system are often unprepared for life on their own. Studies have shown that they are often poorly educated and are less likely to graduate from high school, often due to multiple moves and schools. They also lack the skills to hold a job and be self-sufficient. As one former foster youth explains, "I was never informed what to do when I didn't have a diploma or GED [general equivalency diploma] when I needed to get a job, or even how much work is put into getting a job. Nor was I taught how to fill out an application, what to bring with me to a job interview, the cost to go job hunting . . . or even what to wear to an interview."[54]

As a result, young adults who have recently left foster care are more likely to be unemployed, homeless, addicted to drugs and alcohol, and to spend time in jail. According to a 2017 report by the National Conference of State Legislatures, one in five foster youth who aged out of the system at eighteen was homeless. Only 58 percent had graduated high school by age nineteen, as compared to 87 percent of all nineteen-year-olds. Only 46 percent were employed. And 25 percent were involved in the criminal justice system within two years of aging out of care. These statistics illustrate that many teens are not prepared for life on their own after foster care.

Easing the Transition to Adulthood

To ease the transition out of foster care, federal law requires child welfare agencies to assist foster youth in developing a personalized transition plan. The plan addresses specific options regarding housing, education, finding a job, health insurance, mentoring, and other support services. Caseworkers meet with the teen and other involved adults, such as a foster parent or other mentor, to develop the plan.

Additionally, teens living in foster care are eligible to participate in independent living programs beginning around age fourteen, the age when they would be learning basic life skills from their parents. These programs focus on a variety of topics, ranging from hygiene to opening bank accounts. Although the programs provide valuable information, some teens believe they are too immature at age fourteen to benefit from such information. Htet Htet Rodgers, a twenty-one-year-old former foster youth, says that she completed a state-mandated independent living program before aging out of the system at eighteen, but she still felt unprepared to be on her own after foster care. "It was not engaging to a 14-year-old, nor was it important to me then," she says. "I didn't think it would be worth anything to lodge random information into my head years before I needed it."[55]

To help foster youth better transition to adulthood, several states have extended foster care services until age twenty-one. Enacted in 2008, the Foster Connections to Success and Increasing Adoptions Act is a federal law that gives states federal funding to extend foster care benefits to youth up to age twenty-one. Adding a few extra years to foster care can be very beneficial for youth, giving them more time to mature and more support as they transition into adulthood. The extra years in foster care also keeps them connected to caretakers and foster families. They have more time to find appropriate living situations, which cuts down on the number of homeless foster youth. The extra years of care also give youth a higher chance of graduating from high school or earning a GED. "A child isn't ready at 18. Reality doesn't click in," says Delia Penton, a foster parent. "Legislation should do something to extend it, give them somewhere to go, a foundation, affordable housing so they can get started."[56]

At age eighteen, Jazmin Favela still lives in a foster home, taking care of her two-month-old baby and attending a local community college. She hopes to become a preschool teacher and earn a degree in psychology. To make it easier to achieve her goals, Favela has decided to stay in the foster care system until age twenty-one. "I'm going to stay and receive those services," Favela says. "It's going to be easier for me to get on my feet. If I just jump straight out on my own with my daughter, it'll be hard. I won't be able to support her financially."[57]

To ease the transition to living on their own, young people in foster care can take part in independent living programs. These programs teach basic life skills ranging from how to find housing and jobs to opening bank accounts and maintaining good hygiene.

Some states, such as California, give foster youth in extended care programs the option of choosing among different living situations. Foster youth can choose to live with a host family or in an apartment with a supervising adult. They can also choose to live alone in an apartment with regular contact and supervision from a caseworker. "We've really seen youth take advantage of the opportunity to stay in care, to get continued resources, to make the transition to adulthood a little smoother," says Jennifer Rodriguez, a former foster care recipient and the executive director of the Youth Law Center in San Francisco. "We've offered a lot of young people stability in that period of young adulthood when you realize, 'This is what it's like to be on my own.'"[58]

Finding Support in Many Ways

Being part of a foster family is different for every person. For some, their time in a foster family is brief, a short stay before being reunified with their birth family. Others may live in foster care for years. As foster youth become young adults, there are many places they can turn to for support to help them lead successful and productive lives. For some, this support comes from the relationships they have made in their foster families. For others, support comes from families they create themselves—through friendships, support groups, and other relationships in their lives.

Alec Vanowen entered foster care for the first time at two months old. He joined a family that included biological children,

Building Bridges to Independence

In 2018 Ohio announced the launch of Bridges, a new program to help former foster youth successfully transition to adulthood. Traditionally, teens in Ohio reached the end of foster care at age eighteen. With Bridges, eligible young adults will be able to receive housing and other support services until they are twenty-one. "Few of us have the skills, tools and wisdom we need to live on our own and make informed career decisions when we turn 18," says Cynthia Dungey, the director of the Ohio Department of Job and Family Services. "Bridges will provide the helping hand many youth need during an often turbulent time. It will help former foster youth become successful, self-sufficient adults." In the program, young adults regularly meet with Bridges representatives. During these meetings, they create goals for themselves, learn independent living skills, and can access services to help with finding a job, getting health care, pursuing an education, and more. To continue receiving services from Bridges, young adults must be in school, have a job, be participating in an employment program, or have a medical condition that prevents them from working or getting an education.

Ohio Department of Job and Family Services, "New Bridges Program to Help Former Foster Youth Achieve Independence," February 2, 2018. http://jfs.ohio.gov.

other adopted children, and foster children. "My family accepted me from the second they saw me, and I was blessed to be accepted into a foster-to-adopt home," he says. Eventually, Vanowen's birth parents gave up their parental rights and his foster parents adopted him. He strongly believes that foster care is an important part in building families, whether temporary or permanent. "Foster care

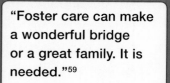

"Foster care can make a wonderful bridge or a great family. It is needed."[59]

—Alec Vanowen, a young man who was adopted by his foster family

can make a wonderful bridge or a great family. It is needed. Our legacy as Americans should be to take care of the thousands of children in foster care no matter what race, number in a sibling group, or what special need the child has. All children deserve families. As permanent as they can be,"[59] he says.

Source Notes

Chapter One: How American Families Are Changing

1. Quoted in Ellen McCarthy, "This Life: To This Foster Mom, Every Child Who Enters Her Home Is 'My Child,'" *Washington Post*, March 27, 2016. www.washingtonpost.com.
2. Quoted in McCarthy, "This Life."
3. Quoted in McCarthy, "This Life."
4. Quoted in Administration for Children, Youth, and Families, "Number of Children in Foster Care Continues to Increase," November 30, 2017. www.acf.hhs.gov.
5. Quoted in Child Welfare Information Gateway, "Reunification: Bringing Your Children Home from Foster Care," May 2016. www.childwelfare.gov.
6. Lisa Marie Basile, "Foster Care Youth: We Are Everyone's & No One's Responsibility," *Huffington Post,* May 19, 2015. www.huffingtonpost.com.
7. Quoted in Administration for Children, Youth, and Families, "Number of Children in Foster Care Continues to Increase."
8. Quoted in University of South Florida, "Growing Opioid Epidemic Forcing More Children into Foster Care," ScienceDaily, January 8, 2018. www.sciencedaily.com.
9. Quoted in SacCounty News, "Foster Parenting—You Can Do It," July 25, 2017. www.saccounty.net.
10. Quoted in Sharon Van Epps, "New Attitudes Toward Adoption from Foster Care Offer Hope," *Washington Post,* July 24, 2017. www.washingtonpost.com.

Chapter Two: How I See Myself and My Family

11. Alexis Griffin, "Surviving the System," Children's Rights, May 2, 2016. www.childrensrights.org.
12. Quoted in Children's Rights, "Meet Edgar Carranza: Foster Youth Advocate," September 29, 2017. www.childrensrights.org.

13. Sophia Williams-Baugh, "They Don't Know the Life of a Foster Child," Children's Rights, May 13, 2016. www.childrens rights.org.
14. Samantha Smith, "Beating the Odds," Children's Rights, June 16, 2017. www.childrensrights.org.
15. Georgette Todd, "What Saved Me in Foster Care," Children's Rights, May 16, 2017. www.childrensrights.org.
16. Quoted in Sarah Marsh, "Our Lives in Foster Care: What It Feels Like to Be Given a New Family," *Guardian* (Manchester, UK), February 12, 2016. www.theguardian.com.
17. John Devine, "Foster Care: The Feeling of Isolation and Overcoming," Children's Rights, May 6, 2016. www.childrens rights.org.
18. Breanna, "Trust," *Voice*, May 2013. www.youthnewsletter.net.
19. Quoted in AdoptUSKids, "Being Loved Has Taught Me How to Love," January 8, 2018. www.adoptuskids.org.
20. Lisa Marie Basile, "A Foster Child of the Opioid Epidemic," *New York Times*, November 24, 2017. www.nytimes.com.
21. Quoted in Meghan Moravcik Walbert, "In a Loving Foster Family, but Missing Home," *New York Times*, March 27, 2018. www.nytimes.com.

Chapter Three: How Others See Me and My Family

22. Margie Fink, "Don't Judge This Child—Chapter 4—Parent Discussion," Transfiguring Adoption, April 20, 2015. http://transfiguringadoption.com.
23. Quoted in Holly Hudson, "In Transition: Teens Aging Out of Foster Care System Battle Stigma, Need Support," *Courier* (Waterloo/Cedar Falls, IA), December 22, 2013. http://wcf courier.com.
24. Quoted in *Chronicle of Social Change*, "Stigma Associated with Youth in the Foster Care System," August 5, 2016. https://chronicleofsocialchange.org.
25. Amma Mante, "8 Things All Kids in Foster Care Want People to Know," Elite Daily, May 15, 2016. www.elitedaily.com.
26. Fink, "Don't Judge This Child."
27. Quoted in Camalott Todd, "Children on the Cusp: The Transition from Foster Care to Adulthood Is Leaving Some Behind," *Las Vegas Sun*, March 13, 2017. https://lasvegassun.com.

28. *Chronicle of Social Change,* "Stigma Associated with Youth in the Foster Care System."
29. Brianna June Wiles, "7 Things That People Don't Tell You About Foster Care or Being Adopted," Odyssey Online, August 22, 2016. www.theodysseyonline.com.
30. Wiles, "7 Things That People Don't Tell You About Foster Care or Being Adopted."
31. Wiles, "7 Things That People Don't Tell You About Foster Care or Being Adopted."
32. Quoted in *Talk of the Nation,* "The Foster Care System: What Parents Wish We Knew," NPR, March 21, 2013. www.npr.org.
33. Chris Chimielewski, "A Special Review of: *The Fosters*," *Foster Focus,* May 2013. www.fosterfocusmag.com.
34. Shalita O'Neale, "How the Mainstream Media Sees Us," *Foster Focus,* November/December 2013. www.fosterfocus mag.com.
35. Quoted in Neda Ulaby, "Foster Families Take Center Stage," *All Things Considered,* June 3, 2013. www.npr.org.
36. Kalyani Gopal, "Changing Perceptions of Foster Care," *Foster Focus*, April 2015. www.fosterfocusmag.com.
37. Gopal, "Changing Perceptions of Foster Care."
38. Barbara, "Perceptions of Youth in Care," *Voice,* May 2013. www.youthnewsletter.net.

Chapter Four: Other People Who Have Families Like Mine

39. Quoted in Chris Chimielewski, "The Rise of Jimmy Graham," *Foster Focus*, August 2012. www.fosterfocusmag.com.
40. Quoted in Chimielewski, "The Rise of Jimmy Graham."
41. Quoted in Jay Moye, "Just a Kid from Goldsboro: Jimmy Graham on His Rise from Group Home to Gridiron Greatness," Coca-Cola Company, September 13, 2015. www.coca-cola company.com.
42. Quoted in Caity Weaver, "There's Something Funny About Tiffany Haddish," *GQ*, March 26, 2018. www.gq.com.
43. Quoted in David Greene, "Tiffany Haddish: 'I Know What I'm Supposed to Do Here on This Earth,'" *Morning Edition*, December 14, 2017. www.npr.org.

44. Quoted in Davina A. Merritt, *Fostering Hope for America.* San Bernardino, CA: Create Space, 2014.
45. Quoted in Ginny Graves, "Jimmy Wayne's Humble Beginnings Were Full of Heartaches," *Good Housekeeping,* October 18, 2016. www.goodhousekeeping.com.
46. Quoted in Graves, "Jimmy Wayne's Humble Beginnings Were Full of Heartaches."
47. Quoted in Graves, "Jimmy Wayne's Humble Beginnings Were Full of Heartaches."

Chapter Five: When Foster Care and Family Ties End

48. Quoted in Deborah Yetter, "Former Foster Care Kids Find Homes Thanks to Nonprofit," *Seattle Times*, December 31, 2017. www.seattletimes.com.
49. Quoted in Yetter, "Former Foster Care Kids Find Homes Thanks to Nonprofit."
50. Quoted in Philippa Law, "Foster Care After 18: Care Leavers Share Their Experiences," *Guardian* (Manchester, UK), January 7, 2014. www.theguardian.com.
51. Quoted in Todd, "Children on the Cusp."
52. LaTasha C. Watts, "Aging Out of Foster Care and into Reality," Children's Rights, May 21, 2017. www.childrensrights.org.
53. Quoted in Baptist Message, "LBCH's PathFinders Expands to Meet Needs of Youth 'Aging Out' of Louisiana Foster Care," April 20, 2015. http://baptistmessage.com.
54. Quoted in Child Welfare Information Gateway, "Helping Youth Transition to Adulthood: Guidance for Foster Parents," April 2013. www.childwelfare.gov.
55. Quoted in Lex Talamo, "Youth Aging Out of Foster Care Struggle to Survive in the 'Real World,'" *Shreveport (LA) Times*, March 12, 2017. www.shreveporttimes.com.
56. Quoted in Talamo, "Youth Aging Out of Foster Care Struggle to Survive in the 'Real World.'"
57. Quoted in Teresa Wiltz, "States Tackle 'Aging Out' of Foster Care," Pew Charitable Trusts, March 25, 2015. www.pewtrusts.org.
58. Quoted in Wiltz, "States Tackle 'Aging Out' of Foster Care."
59. Alec Vanowen, "Real Stories: Alec Vanowen's Foster Care Story," Foster More, October 6, 2017. https://fostermore.org.

For Further Research

Books

Cris Beam, *To the End of June: The Intimate Life of American Foster Care.* New York: Houghton Mifflin Harcourt, 2014.

Leanne Currie-McGhee, *Foster Youth*. San Diego: Reference-Point, 2017.

Rosie Lewis and Casey Watson, *Angels in Our Hearts: A Moving Collection of True Fostering Stories.* New York: HarperCollins, 2018.

Joyce Libal, *The Foster Care System (Living with a Special Need).* Broomall, PA: Mason Crest, 2014.

Catherine E. Rymph, *Raising Government Children: A History of Foster Care and the American Welfare State*. Chapel Hill: University of North Carolina Press, 2017.

Jimmy Wayne, *Walk to Beautiful: The Power of Love and a Homeless Kid Who Found the Way.* Nashville: Thomas Nelson, 2014.

Internet Sources

Children's Rights, "Finding My Way: Childhood Memories of Foster Care," September 2016. www.childrensrights.org/wp-content/uploads/2017/03/CR-Blog-Brochure-2016-9.26_single-lowres.pdf.

Child Welfare Information Gateway, "Foster Care Statistics 2016," April 2018. www.childwelfare.gov/pubPDFs/foster.pdf#page=4&view=Placement.

Child Welfare Information Gateway, "Helping Youth Transition to Adulthood: Guidance for Foster Parents," April 2013. www.childwelfare.gov/pubPDFs/youth_transition.pdf.

US Department of Health and Human Services, "The AFCARS Report Preliminary FY 2016 Estimates as of Oct. 20, 2017," 2017. www.acf.hhs.gov/sites/default/files/cb/afcarsreport24.pdf.

Organizations and Websites

Children's Rights (www.childrensrights.org). Children's Rights is a nonprofit organization that advocates for youth in the foster care system. Its website provides fact sheets and other information about foster care, aging out, finding a permanent family, and more.

Child Welfare Information Gateway (www.childwelfare.gov). The Child Welfare Information Gateway is part of the Children's Bureau within the US Department of Health and Human Services. Its website provides the latest news and information related to foster care, including numerous publications, links to websites, state guides and resources, and more.

FosterClub (www.fosterclub.com). FosterClub provides a peer support network for children and youth in foster care. Its website offers information and fact sheets about foster care, real-life stories, and links to state-based resources for foster youth.

Together We Rise (www.togetherwerise.org). Together We Rise is a nonprofit organization dedicated to improving the lives of youth in foster care. Its website has information about the various programs developed to benefit foster youth.

Index